★ ★ ★

MONTREAL
Expos

JAMES R. ROTHAUS

CREATIVE EDUCATION

Library of Congress Cataloging-in-Publication Data

Rothaus, James.
  Montreal Expos.

  Summary: A history of the first major league
baseball team to play in Canada.
   1. Montreal Expos (Baseball team) — History — Juvenile
literature.   [1. Montreal Expos (Baseball team) — History.
2. Baseball — History]   I. Title.
GV875.M6R   1987   796.357'64'09714281   87-22219
ISBN 0-88682-142-8

★ ★ ★

CONTENTS

The Great Adventure Begins (1968) 7
The "Little General" Leads Expos
    Through Their First Campaign 8
Baseball Fever Spreads (1970-73) 14
New Faces In The Clubhouse (1974-76) 20
Dick Williams Launches Big Turnaround 24
A Run At The Championship (1979-80) 29
The First Title (1981) 33
The Big Thud (1982-84) 37
Injury Bug Bites Rodgers 38
Raising The Roof (1987) 45

COVER PHOTO
Hubie Brooks on the move in
the dog days of the
1986 campaign.

PHOTO SPREAD (PAGE 2/3)
So close! Montreal's
Andres Galarraga nearly nabs
Milt Thompson of Philly on the
pickoff play. (1987)

This is the story of the Montreal Expos—the first major league baseball team to play in Canada. The story of the Expos is the story of fascinating men like Rusty Staub, Bill "Stony" Stoneman, Mike Marshall, Steve Rogers, Gary Carter, Andre Dawson, Tim Raines and many other outstanding players. It is the story of how a single team turned an entire country onto baseball.

Sure, hockey is the national sport of Canada. In fact, the Montreal Canadians are one of the most legendary hockey teams in the world. Many times over the years it has won the Stanley Cup for being the best team in the entire National Hockey League.

The Expos, on the other hand, have captured just one Division Championship, and have yet to make their first trip to the World Series. Still, the Expos fans love and respect their team just as much as the city's hockey fans love and respect the Canadians. This book will show you why.

The Great Adventure Begins (1968)

For years, a group of baseball-starved Montreal businessmen had been trying to persuade major league baseball to come to their city in Canada. In 1960, the league granted Montreal a minor league team, but the fans didn't support it. They didn't want the minor leagues, they wanted the real thing . . . the big leagues!

It seemed that each time the businessmen asked for a team, they got the same answers back from the league. "It's too cold up there," or "Hockey is number one in Canada, baseball will never catch on."

One day, Montreal Mayor Jean Drapeau decided that he had heard enough. He knew in his own heart that the

1967
The city of Montreal hosts Expo '67, a World's Fair that focuses international attention on the city and convinces major league baseball to grant a N.L. expansion club to Montreal.

PHOTO
Gary "Big Bat" Carter may be a future Hall-of-Famer.

people of his city loved baseball. He knew that they dreamed of having a major league club of their own. So he put together a plan to get them one.

In 1967, the city of Montreal held a gigantic World's Fair, called "Expo 67." Millions of people from all over the world visited the beautiful city of Montreal to see the Fair. When they left, most of the tourists had a new appreciation for the city itself.

After the World's Fair, Montreal was viewed by the rest of the world as a great metropolis. For such a city, anything and everything seemed possible including a major league baseball team!

On a beautiful spring morning in 1968, Mayor Drapeau's dream finally came true when the National League accepted Montreal's bid to join the big leagues. The team would be called — what else — the "Expos," and it would be the first big league club to ever play in Canada. It also became the first team in baseball to have its game-day program printed in *both* English and French!

It was the beginning of a great adventure — one that would see the Expos battle and scrap their way from the position of worst team in the league to one of the very best.

The "Little General" Leads
Expos Through Their First Campaign

The first step for Montreal President John McHale was to find a manager for his new team. McHale was a seasoned baseball man with 20 years experience. He knew how to find just the right man to lead the new team.

After checking several American cities, McHale finally found the man he was looking for in Philadelphia. His name was Gene "Little General" Mauch.

Mauch had been manager of the Philadelphia Phillies for eight and a half years before coming to Montreal. He was a stern man who insisted that his players follow strict rules. There was no fooling around when Mauch was on the field.

Mauch loved to talk. On the field, in the dugout, in the parking lot after practice — you could always find him chattering away to somebody.

The only time that anybody can remember Gene Mauch being speechless is the first time he saw Montreal's colorful new uniforms. In those days, baseball caps were expected to be drab and simple. But Montreal had chosen a bright red, white and blue cap that was alive with color. The Montreal owners expected their team to have personality and flare.

Mauch put the Expos' cap on his head and got right to work. Coaches and staff were hired. Jarry Stadium, a rickety old place, was renovated, painted and expanded. The excitement was building fast.

By the time the baseball draft rolled around on October 14, 1968, Montreal was a city that was caught up in baseball fever. Clustered around their radios, the Montreal fans listened intently as their very first big league players were selected . . . Mike Wegener, Maury Wills, Jim "Mud Cat" Grant, Carl Morton, Jose "Coco" Laboy, and Bill Stoneman.

The excitement continued through the fall of '68, as Gene Mauch picked and traded his players. Old-timers and rookies tried out under his watchful eye. On the 22nd of January, 1969, Mauch made his biggest trade of

Apr. 17, 1969
Montreal ace
Stony Stoneman
pitches the club's
first no-hitter.

PHOTO
After a two-day retirement, Maury Wills (30) puts on his uniform again and warms up with his Expos teammates. (1969)

all. This particular player's name was Rusty Staub, but the French-speaking people in Montreal immediately nicknamed him "Le Grand Orange" because of his fiery red hair. In no time at all, Staub would become the Expos' first true superstar.

In April of 1969, the Expos headed to West Palm Beach, Florida, for spring training. Up in Montreal, the stadium was nearing completion, and the entire city was getting ready to greet their Expos. But when the team finally arrived back in town from sunny Florida, they ran into one big problem.

Snow! That's right . . . even in April a thick blanket of Canadian snow covered the baselines at Jarry Field. Maybe the pessimists had been right. Maybe it *was* too cold in Montreal to play baseball.

"No way," yelled the fans. "Let's shovel off the snow and play ball!"

Rusty Staub warmed things up with a red-hot hitting streak that started on the opening night. Home runs, triples, doubles, RBIs — Staub hit 'em all. On opening night Staub, Dan McGuin and Coco Laboy all drove homers into the outfield bleachers. That night, the Expos tallied 11 runs against the New York Mets, but that was just the beginning.

Three nights later, April 17, Bill Stoneman pitched himself into the record books. That night, Stony hurled a no-hit, no-run game against the Philadelphia Phillies. Imagine! The Expos were less than a month old and already they were pitching no-hitters against the awesome old Philadelphia Phillies.

For Stony it was a dream come true. As a kid growing up in Illinois, he had pictured himself on a big-league mound, mowing down rank after rank of enemy batters.

1969
The Expos record a string of 10 games in which they hit one or more homers in each game.

PHOTO
Roy Face was an inspiration to young Expos rookies in 1969.

Now the no-hitter was a reality!

At first, Stony and the other American-born players felt uncomfortable in Canada. Because so many of the Montreal fans spoke French, the players used to carry little pocket dictionaries so they could understand what was being said. Rusty Staub felt embarrassed the day he received a fan letter and couldn't read it because it was in French. A group of brand-new players on a brand-new team in a town that didn't always speak English—it all added up to a difficult first year.

Of course, that's how it usually is in baseball. First-year teams don't win too many games, and Montreal was no exception.

After finishing the first season with 52 wins and 110 losses, Mauch summed up the season like this: "Oh, sure, we figure to get knocked around pretty often at first. But we'll win plenty of ball games. I was really surprised by the crowds in Montreal (the team drew 1,212,608 its first season). I expected noise, but I didn't expect the games to be so important to them. I really felt touched."

Baseball Fever Spreads (1970-73)

The next year—1971—Mauch really lived up to his nickname. The "Little General" held one of the toughest spring training sessions ever. "At the end of each day, I felt like an old sock in a washing machine," grumbled one Expos outfielder. Still, it was just what the Expos seemed to need. The batting got sharper, the pitching improved, and the spirit of the team simply soared.

On the opening day of 1970, veteran pitcher Claude

Raymond revved up his tired old arm and kept it revved for the rest of the season. If one of the young Expos pitchers got into trouble, Mauch would simply summon Raymond from the bullpen. Twenty-three times Raymond saved the Expos that year. It would be the best year of his entire career.

Of course, starting pitcher Carl Morton didn't seem to need Raymond's help too much in 1970. Morton, a rookie righthander wound up with an outstanding 18-11 record — good enough to be named as the National League's Rookie of the Year. He was also voted the Expos Player of the Year.

The Expos did so well in 1970 that many of the old hockey fans started going to the baseball games. Out at the ballpark the fans would sit in the warm summer sun and cheer for their team. The French-speaking Canadians shouted out "*Vive les Expos*" (long live the Expos) when their team started a rally.

There were many big moments in the 1970 season. Like the time Rusty Staub hit four home runs in a doubleheader against the Dodgers. Or the times Ron Hunt made it to first by failing to get out of the way of an incoming fastball.

It seems that Hunt had a knack for getting hit by the pitch. He led the league in that category every year for seven years. Some of the players said he was crazy to step in front of 90-mph fastballs. But Hunt didn't seem to mind too much. He just trotted down to first base, listening to the cheers in Jarry Park. Over his entire career Hunt would get hit a total of 243 times!

By the end of the 1970 season, the Expos had won 73 games and lost 89. Mauch's prediction of winning over 70 games in 1970 had come true. The Expos were defi-

1971
Ouch!
Ron Hunt is hit by a record 50 pitches in a single season.

PHOTO
Swarmin' Warren.
It was batting practice, 1980, and Warren Cromartie showed the intensity that helped spark the team.

nitely a team on the move.

It was in 1971 that the rest of the National League teams really started taking notice of the Expos. Like a stern Army drill sergeant, Mauch kept his team in line. The discipline paid off, too, as the Expos outhustled, out-pitched and out-hit some of the best teams in baseball, including the New York Mets, the St. Louis Cardinals, the Philadelphia Phillies and more. In reality, the Expos were the straightest, most disciplined team on the field that year, and respect comes naturally to such a team.

Rusty Staub, "Le Grand Orange," hit well again in 1971. Already he was Canada's number one baseball hero. On the field, he hit with power and style. Off the field, he was the perfect gentleman. By the end of the '71 season, Rusty had a total of 78 homers and 270 runs in his three years with the Expos.

Before the start of the '72 season, however, Mauch shocked all of Montreal when he announced that Canada's hero, Rusty Staub, had been traded to the Mets for Mike Jorgensen, Tim Foli and Ken Singleton.

Actually, the experts agreed that it was a pretty good trade. As the '72 season took shape, Singleton picked up where Staub left off, winning the hearts of Expos fans with his powerful hitting and flawless fielding.

Tim "Crazy Horse" Foli moved right in and locked down the shortstop spot.

With Singleton driving in runs, and Foli sparking the double plays, Mauch turned his eye to the pitching staff.

Mike Marshall, the wise old hurler who had come to the Expos in 1970, was considered one of the top relief pitchers in the game by '72.

Bill Stoneman threw his second no-hitter on October 2, and the Expos continued to build a winning reputation all through the spring and summer of '72.

No, the Expos didn't win the pennant or World Series that year, but they did provide the loyal Expos fans with 70 victories and some of the most action-packed games in baseball history.

When spring training, 1973 rolled around, everyone could see Mike Marshall was up to something special.

After working hard all winter, Marshall showed up at camp with more zip on his fastball and more curve on his curveball. Nobody, it seemed, could hit him.

When the season opened, Marshall started off on a hot streak. Batter after batter went down to defeat. Whenever Stony Stoneman, Steve Rogers or any of the other Montreal pitchers would get into a bind, the fans immediately chanted for Marshall. That season Mike appeared on the mound in 92 games (a team record) and saved 31 games (also a team record).

Yup, 1973 was quite a season. Gene Mauch was named Manager of the Year for leading the Expos to within 3-1/2 games of first place in the Eastern division. Along the way there had been plenty of fireworks.

Outfielder Bob "Beetles" Bailey drove in more than 60 runs. Ken Singleton was outstanding down the stretch, robbing batter after batter of certain base hits. Tim Foli surpassed everyone's expectations. And Mauch . . . well, all he could do was smile.

"Wait until next year," he said with a gleam in his eye. "These guys are just getting started."

New Faces In The Clubhouse (1974-76)

Before the end of 1973, Mauch made a bold move to

1975
Ken Singleton,
Ron Fairly and
Willie Davis are
swapped for rookies
Larry Parrish and
Gary Carter. Carter
plays in the All-Star
game and is voted
team MVP. Mauch is
replaced at season's
end after his seventh
year with the Expos.

bring more power to the Expos lineup. Mike Marshall was traded to the Dodgers for outfielder Willie Davis. Though the fans thought it was a bad trade, Davis proved them wrong.

Willie stepped right into the Expos starting lineup and let 'er rip. All season long his clutch hits and tricky base-stealing inspired the team. More than once, Davis drove in the game-winning run with a towering late-inning homer. With Davis leading the way, the Expos charged through the 1974 season.

When it was over, the team had set records for hitting, pitching and winning. In 153 games, Davis batted .295, had 48 extra base hits, drove in 89 runs and stole 25 bases. The year ended with the Expos standing at 79 wins, 82 losses—their best season ever.

When the vote was taken for 1974 MVP, Davis won easily. By 1975, baseball fever was so intense in Montreal that tickets were scarce for most of the home games. It seemed that the whole city wanted to watch the Expos. The Expos fans were the loudest in all of baseball.

During 1975 the Expos began a vigorous rebuilding program. Mauch and General Manager Jim Fanning had their own ideas about the "right combination" of veterans and young players, but some of their decisions were difficult for the fans to accept.

In order to make room for younger players, Ken Singleton, Ron Fairly and Willie Davis said good-bye. In their place, Mauch brought two promising rookies up from the Expos farm club. Their names were Larry Parrish and Gary Carter. It was history in the making.

Though Parrish and Carter were just rookies in 1975, they hit like seasoned veterans. Parrish ripped 10 home runs and drove in 65 RBIs his first season. Carter hit a phenomenal 17 home runs and knocked in 68 RBIs.

From the beginning, Mauch knew he had a player of great potential in Gary Carter. The tall, handsome California kid was the talk of Montreal. Carter had a way of making the fans proud of the entire team. In his rookie season Carter was voted into the All-Star game. He was also voted the team's MVP in his first season.

Because of the rebuilding in '75, the team slipped to its worst record in four years. The "Little General" won 75 games while losing 87.

When the season ended, team president John McHale decided it was time for a change. He fired Gene Mauch and replaced him with Karl Kuehl. The reign of the "Little General" was over. After seven seasons with the team, Mauch left with a record of 499 wins and 627 losses. He left knowing that he had done his part in helping an entire country catch baseball fever.

While Americans were celebrating the Bicentennial in the summer of 1976, Montreal was going through its most embarrassing season. The eyes of the world were focused on Montreal that summer because that's where the Summer Olympics were being held. The Expos did not put on a very good show. Even the fans walked out on their team in the summer of '76. Attendance dropped from an all-time high of 1,424,683 in 1970 to only 646,704. Nothing seemed to go right that summer.

The Expos continued to lose, game after game, week after week. Carter dropped from 17 home runs to six. Pitcher Steve Rogers won only seven games and lost 17.

The only two players who really shined in '76 were pinch-hitter Jose Morales and pitcher Woodie Fryman. In truth, the team seemed to miss the "Little General."

1977
The Expos move into mammoth Olympic Stadium. Manager Dick Williams rallies the club to 20 more victories than the year before. Ellis Valentine is named N.L. Rookie of the Year. Rookie Andre Dawson booms 19 homers.

The Expos slid downhill so fast in '76 that manager Karl Kuehl was fired in September and Expos scout Charlie Fox was made manager for the last few games. No matter. By then, Montreal was on the road to its worst finish in seven years. They won only 55 games that year, while losing 107. Ah, but even that cloud had a silver lining.

Dick Williams Launches Big Turnaround

The 1977 season started off with a big bang for the Expos. President McHale announced that Dick Williams had been hired as the new manager. Williams was a fiery coach who challenged his players, squawked at umpires and won lots of ball games.

In 1972 and '73 Williams had guided the Oakland A's to two straight World Championships. Now he was in Montreal.

To add another dash of excitement the Expos now moved into Olympic Stadium — the huge 60,000-seat stadium that had been built for the Summer Olympics.

With Williams leading the way, the '77 season was the beginning of the Expos big turnaround. One of Williams' first jobs was to put veteran players on his roster. Before the '77 season started, he had picked up hot-hitting Dave Cash from the Phillies and RBI man Tony Perez from the Reds. These two added much-needed power to the Expos lineup.

Once the season began, Cash, Perez, Carter and Parrish all had hot bats. Pitcher Steve Rogers put together one of his finest seasons ever. But the surprise of the year was the outstanding play of three young Expos — Ellis Valentine, Andre Dawson and Warren Cromartie.

PHOTO
Looks easy.
Lefty Ross Grimsley
made it look very
easy as he fired his
third victory
without a loss
in 1979.

Valentine, a stocky outfielder, had 149 hits and 25 home runs in only his second season. Dawson surprised everybody in his rookie season when he belted 25 home runs and had 72 RBIs. His hitting earned him 1977 National League Rookie of the Year honors. The runner-up was teammate Warren Cromartie who had 175 hits and 50 RBIs in his first season.

All through the season Williams worked to blend the deep experience of players like Cash and Perez with the raw power of Carter, Parrish, Valentine and Dawson. Williams was convinced that his team would soon be ready to take a run at the National League Championship.

The Expos' tenth year, 1978, opened with high hopes in Florida. Over the winter Williams had picked up lefthanders Ross Grimsley and Rudy May to add more depth to his pitching staff.

"Grimsley and May are just what the doctor ordered," Williams said. "With four bona fide starters, we know we'll be able to win the close ones."

With Dave Cash batting .289 at second, Tony Perez holding down first with a .283 average and Gary Carter belting 31 home runs, the Expos had plenty of punch in the '78 season. Cromartie, Dawson and Valentine were quickly becoming the best outfield in baseball. All the ingredients were there to make Montreal serious pennant contenders. Then bad luck struck.

Though the hitting was strong in '78, the pitching seemed jinxed all season. In late July, Rudy May fell and broke his ankle. From then on, the Expos struggled on the mound.

One night in Atlanta the Expos did something that made them forget all their troubles. Against Atlanta, on

PHOTO
A rare photo of
Pete "Charlie Hustle"
Rose in an Expos
uniform. (1984)

26

July 30, Toronto set a team record by belting out eight home runs.

But that was one of the few real highlights of the season. When the final game ended, the Expos had sputtered to a 76-86 record, good for only fourth place.

Immediately, the Expos launched a special four-point improvement program. By improving the team's speed, catching, bench strength and bullpen, the Expos felt they could squeeze out more wins. The fans held their breath.

A Run At The Championship (1979-80)

In '79, the Expos added pitcher Bill "The Spaceman" Lee and speedster Ron LeFlore to the lineup. These two players were the missing ingredients.

When the season opened on April 19, the Expos were off and running. They won 14 of their first 19 games. By the end of May the Expos led the majors in winning percentage (.750) and were on top of the National League in batting with a .284 team average.

It looked like the championship season the Expos had sought for so long. At the plate, Dawson, Valentine and Cromartie unleashed a torrent of home runs, grand slams and sizzling liners.

Bill "The Spaceman" Lee was kind of crazy. He'd been known to wear a gas mask, coonskin cap or even a beanie out to the mound. That didn't bother Williams. After all, Lee went 16-10, had a 3.04 ERA and was voted to the *Sporting News* All-Star Team.

Through the long, hot summer the Expos were even with the Pirates. Through August and September they hung on. The fans were convinced that the champion-

1979
Pitcher Dave Palmer wins eight in a row. Steve Rogers throws five shutouts. Both are all-time club records.

PHOTO
Not Valentine's day. Ellis Valentine (17) got caught for a change between bases. (1978)

1980
The Expos record
their second straight
second-place finish.
Ron LeFlore sets an
all-time club record
by pilfering 97 bases.
Andre Dawson
scatters 17
game-winning RBIs.

PHOTO
Smooth-fielding
Tim Wallach
contributed 71 RBIs
for the Expos in '86.

ship dream was about to come true.

Going down the stretch, the Expos trailed by only two games, but the red-hot Phillies left them two games short of the title.

The Montreal fans were disappointed. Never in the team's history had they come so close to winning the division. The 95-65 record was by far the best in the team's history.

A few months later the experts said the 1980 Expos were a team on the verge of something big. Six of the starting eight players were entering their prime playing days. The lineup featured the best catcher (Gary Carter) and the best centerfielder (Andre Dawson) in the league. Carter had hit 29 homers, drove in 101 runs and won a Gold Glove award in '79. Dawson had batted .308 with 87 RBIs and stolen 34 bases the same season.

Rounding out the Expos powerhouse lineup were Larry Parrish, Rodney Scott, Warren Cromartie, Chris Speier, Ron LeFlore and Ellis Valentine.

The pitching was excellent in '80, too. Any of the first three starters — Steve Rogers, Scott Sanderson and Bill Gullickson — had the arm to win 20 games.

From the first game of the season the Expos were off like a shot. LeFlore sparked the running game with 97 thefts, including 22 straight steals.

Early in the season, on May 10, French-born Charlie Lea became only the third pitcher in Expos history to throw a no-hitter. The French-Canadian crowd cheered especially loud for their hero.

In the first week of September pitcher Steve Rogers beat the Mets, 3-0, to record his 100th career win. The very next night, 21-year old rookie sensation Bill Gullickson struck out 18 batters to beat the Cubs, 4-2. It

was a club record and one shy of the National League record of 19 strikeouts in a single game.

The rest of the '80 season went the same way. Carter, Dawson, and Valentine powered in the runs. LeFlore stole bases. Montreal starting pitcher Scott Sanderson came on strong in the late season and won 16 games.

For the second year in a row, Montreal and Philadelphia battled neck-and-neck for the title. It came down to the final weekend before the race was decided.

But the Phillies rode into town for the second year in a row and beat the Expos twice to win the division. The Expos were brokenhearted. The Phillies would go on to win the World Series.

The First Title (1981)

The 1981 season started with fans, managers and players talking about a possible baseball strike—the first strike in the history of the game.

That didn't slow down the Expos, though. They streaked ahead, even though the master base-stealer— Ron LeFlore—had been traded to Chicago during the off season. Some said the Expos' running game was gone, but then rookie Tim Raines came to town.

"Rock" Raines could run like a gazelle. He stepped right into LeFlore's shoes and took off sprinting. He broke LeFlore's base-stealing record when he stole 27 straight times without being caught. Instantly, he was the Expos' big star. Raines helped the team get off to its best start ever.

Then the bottom fell out. The baseball strike stopped Raines and the Expos dead in their tracks. For weeks and weeks, the players and owners argued back and

1981
Rookie Tim Raines joins the club. The Expos win their first division championship in a season marred by a league-wide players' strike.

PHOTO
Perez puts one over. First sacker Tony Perez rockets one over the left-field wall. (1978)

forth. It seemed to go on forever.

Finally, "Play Ball!" was heard again. The first game after the strike was the All-Star Game. Expos catcher Gary Carter proved that night that the long wait hadn't cooled his hot bat. In the All-Star Game he banged two homers and won the MVP award. The Expos were rolling!

For the third year in a row the Expos and Phillies battled down to the wire for the division title. This time the Expos would not be denied.

With Carter leading the hitters, and Rogers sparking the pitching, the Expos went into the playoffs and whipped the World Champion Phillies. For the first time in the history of baseball, the National League Eastern Division Championship was brought north of the border to Canada. *"Vive les Expos!"* Bring on the Dodgers!

The Dodgers and Expos squared off in October to decide the National League Pennant. It was a see-saw series. First, L.A. won, 5-1, then Montreal came back, 3-0. The series moved to chilly Montreal, and the Expos rolled to a 4-1 victory. Back and forth they battled. Carter hit a brilliant .438, but the Dodgers came back with Burt Hooton and rookie sensation Fernando Valenzuela to capture the series, three games to two. Once again, the dejected Expos had to settle for second best.

Even though Montreal lost, the Expos fans stood and cheered for their team long after the game ended. The fans were hooked on the Expos. Win or lose, they would always be loyal fans.

But fan loyalty was to undergo its first major test.

PHOTO
The ever-popular
Al Oliver tips his
cap to the fans in '83.

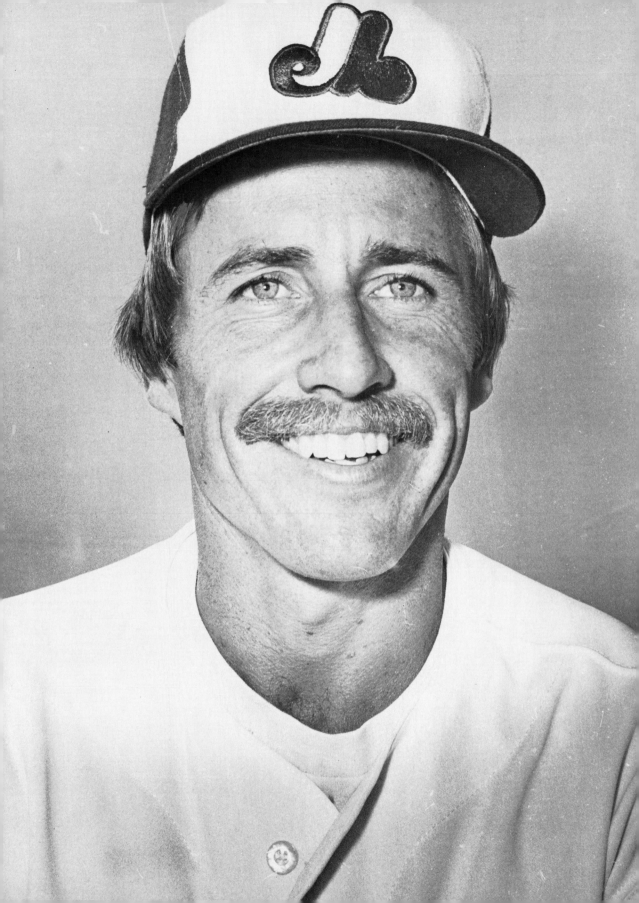

The Big Thud (1982-84)

After their two big seasons of 1980 and '81, the Expos were being hailed nationwide as THE team of the Eighties.

Then something strange occurred. Just before the start of the 1982 campaign, the Expos decided to trade third baseman Larry Parrish and slugger Dave Hostetler to the Texas Rangers in exchange for outfielder Al Oliver. The trade looked okay on paper, but it backfired on Montreal.

Though Oliver was an explosive hitter (he would go on to win the 1982 N.L. batting championship for the Expos), he had lost the powerful throwing arm that brought him Gold Glove honors in the past. No problem, thought Manager Jim Fanning. We'll move Oliver to first base, send first baseman Terry Francona to right field, and move rightfielder Tim Wallach to third where Larry Parrish used to play. If that sounds confusing to you, imagine how confusing it was for Oliver, Francona and Wallach!

More experiments followed. As the season wore on, Tim Raines (the Expos' rookie outfield sensation of 1981) was moved in to second base. At that point, the Expos' lineup consisted of a pitcher, catcher, shortstop, three outfielders . . . plus, three more outfielders disguised as infielders. Now everyone was confused.

As usual, the big Montreal bats thundered that year. Catcher Gary Carter boomed 29 homers. Centerfielder Andre Johnson launched 23. Oliver crunched 22. All the confusion on defense, however, finally dragged the mighty Expos down to third place. Disappointed and

1982
Al Oliver sets an all-time club record with 204 hits—enough to win the N.L. batting title.

PHOTO
Pitcher David Palmer had a lot to smile about in 1979.

frustrated, Manager Jim Fanning threw in the towel on the last day of the season. Bill Virdon would take over as skipper in '83.

As for the fans, they passed their first loyalty test with flying colors. More than 2.3 million spectators — a new high — had shown up to watch the Expos thud into third. More tests were yet to come.

Over the next two seasons — 1983 and '84 — the Expos proved again and again that they had all the talent necessary to sweep through the league.

"Talent, talent, talent — we've got so doggone much talent, but nothing to show for it," fumed Virdon, the new manager, and he was right. The Expos had the gloves, the bats, the arms, the speed, the desire, the excellent front office staff, the fabulous farm system, certainly some of the greatest fans in the majors. Everything. Simply everything. But they still finished third in '83 and — *gulp*! — fifth in '84.

Well, what would *you* do if you owned a team like that? At the end of 1984, the Montreal front office did what most clubs do. Even though the manager is competent, you fire him. Then you issue a news release that praises the guy, but you explain that maybe a new manager might change "the chemistry" of the team.

The decision was okay with Virdon. "I was going to resign anyway," he said.

PHOTO
Gary Carter, a big-time leader of men, calling the shots for the Expos pitching staff. (1986)

Injury Bug Bites Rodgers . . . But Rodgers Bites Back (1985-86)

So, the Expos had yet another new manager in 1985. Buck Rodgers was his name. He was their fourth skipper in four seasons, but he had every intention of stick-

ing around for awhile.

The scouting report on Rodgers pegged him as a shrewd guy who could get more out of less than any other skipper in the majors. He was supposed to be a particular master at using his pitching staff, especially his bullpen. Good thing, too, because the Expos' pitching staff was going to need all the expert guidance it could get.

You see, during 1985, eight of the Expos' pitchers were zapped by major injury. Charlie Lea, a sure 15-game winner, went down for the season. Gary Lucas, Bill Gullickson, Joe Hesketh, David Palmer, Bert Roberge, Dan Schatzer, Bryn Smith and Jeff Reardon also visited the injury list at least once during the year.

Thanks to expert juggling by Rodgers, however, the Expos still moved up two pegs in the standings to finish a very respectable third for the season.

Sure enough, the scouting report on Rodgers had been accurate. Despite all the injuries, pitching was the team's strong point. Rodgers' bullpen had sizzled for 53 saves, the most in the National League. Give special credit there to Jeff "The Terminator" Reardon who led the league with 41 saves and was crowned the N.L. Fireman of the Year.

Before we leave the '85 campaign, let's turn a well-deserved spotlight on leftfielder Tim Raines, shortstop Hubie Brooks, and rightfielder Andre Dawson.

Raines was Mr. Everything that year for the offense. He batted .320, stole 70 bases, scored 115 runs, clubbed 13 triples and 11 homers. When he wasn't swatting balls or stealing bases, you would find him in the dugout, walking from player to player, dishing out high-fives and constant encouragement.

1983
Charlie Lea matches the club record by pitching eight straight victories.

PHOTO
Robbing Rusty. Andre Dawson charges in to rob former Expos star Rusty Staub of an extra base hit in 1981 action against the Mets.

PHOTO
Andy McGaffigan
prepares the slider in
one of his 16
victories for the
Expos in '86.

Hubie Brooks, who had been swapped to the Expos for Gary Carter after the '84 season, batted .269 with 34 doubles and 13 homers. He also accounted for 100 RBIs, the most by a N.L. shortstop since 1960!

Finally, Andre Dawson launched 23 homers and 91 RBIs on the way to winning his sixth Gold Glove award in the outfield.

Manager Rodgers had the perfect one-liner to sum up a season that could have been the "big one," had it not been plagued by injuries. "We could've won it all," he said with a sigh, "but we ran out of pitchers."

The injury bug was back in 1986, but this time he brought his big brother along. You had to feel sorry for Buck Rodgers. So many of his key players were injured in '86 that the fans started making up medical jokes to ease the tension.

Question: What is big, white, has a red cross on the side, and speeds through the streets of Montreal with a siren blaring?

Answer: The Expos team bus!

Question: What's the most successful baseball promotion in Expos' history?

Answer: Free stethoscopes to the first 10,000 fans!

Question: Which two major league records did the Expos break in the 1986 campaign?

Answer: Broken bats and broken bones!

At one point late in the season, a reporter asked Rodgers to name the players on the disabled list. "It would be a lot easier if I just named the guys who *aren't* on the list," said Rodgers, shaking his head.

Without detailing their injuries, the sidelined players included Hubie Brooks, Mike Fitzgerald, Bryn Smith, third baseman Tim Wallach, pitcher Joe Hesketh,

second baseman Vance Law, rookie first baseman Andres Galarraga — and those were just the players with *major* injuries.

It would've been easy for Rodgers and his wounded warriors to throw in the towel. Instead, they leaned on each other for strength and rallied for a respectable (78-83) fourth-place season.

The outfield did its part, that's for sure. Together, Tim Raines, Mitch Webster and Andre Dawson produced a better batting average, and more hits (502), doubles (98) and triples (25) than any other club in the National League. Raines won the N.L. batting crown, stealing 70 bases along the way. Those were among the few bright spots, however.

Now, let's check the fans' performance in '86. *Hmmm.* Some low grades on the loyalty test this time. Home attendance sunk to 1.1 million, the Expos' lowest turnout in ten seasons.

The fewer the fans, the less money the team makes. The less money they make, the less they can afford to hold on to their big stars. And the more big stars they lose, the weaker the club, and the fewer fans. Clearly, the club that started the decade as the "Team of the Eighties" was now a club in dire need of a pick-me-up.

Raising The Roof (1987)

A proud new addition awaited the Expos at the start of the 1987 season. Thanks to a long-awaited construction project, beautiful Olympic Stadium had now become beautiful Olympic "Domed" Stadium.

Along with the new roof, there were several new faces. Gone were superstars Andre Dawson, Tim Raines

Sept. 24, 1985
The Expos score an all-time club high 12 runs in a single inning against Chicago.

PHOTO
The old and the new. Veteran Woodie Fryman (left) and rookie Bill Gullickson team up in spring training. (1981)

and Jeff Reardon. A platoon of hard-charging kids and wily old veterans came in to spring training to scrap for the open positions.

Among the most promising was Floyd Everett Youmans, Jr., 22, proud owner of the most terrifying right arm in Canada. Nearly every one of Youmans' pitches whistled in at more than 90 mph, and he was still a growing boy!

Backing up veteran Hubie Brooks at shortstop was another budding superstar, Luis Rivera, whose fielding in spring training dazzled Manager Rodgers.

The other bright spot in the infield was first baseman Andres "The Giant" Galarraga, the 25-year-old slugger who had bashed five of his first six homers off former Cy Young winners the year before.

Okay, we saved the best 'til last. We were just fooling about Tim Raines leaving the team. After some complicated contract negotiations, Raines returned to the roster in early May and—guess what? He nearly raised the new roof off Olympic Stadium by getting a walk, a single, a steal and a grand-slam home run in his first game back!

There he was in the dugout again, too, walking from player to player, dishing out high-five's and constant encouragement. Just like the good old days. As far as Raines, Rodgers and the Expos are concerned, *these* are the good old days!

PHOTO
Mr. Inspiration!
Tim Raines
was already
emerging as the
Expos' superstar
when this shot was
taken in 1983.